HIDE & SPEAK
FRENCH

Catherine Bruzzone and Susan Martineau
French adviser: Claudine Bharadia
Illustrated by Louise Comfort

b small publishing

À la ferme - On the farm

1	**Le chat** court après **la souris**.	1	**The cat** is chasing **the mouse**.
2	**Le chien** dort au soleil.	2	**The dog** is sleeping in the sun.
3	**Le cheval** est dans l'écurie.	3	**The horse** is in the stable.
4	**La vache** donne du lait.	4	**The cow** gives milk.
5	**Le cochon** mange beaucoup!	5	**The pig** is eating a lot!
6	**Les moutons** sont dans le pré.	6	**The sheep** are in the field.
7	**Le canard** nage sur l'étang.	7	**The duck** is swimming on the pond.
8	**La chèvre** mange de l'herbe.	8	**The goat** is eating grass.

	le chat *ler shah*
	la souris *lah soo-<u>ree</u>*
	le chien *ler shee-<u>yah</u>*
	le cheval *ler sh-<u>val</u>*
	la vache *lah vash*
	le cochon *ler koh-<u>shoh</u>*
	le mouton *ler moo-<u>toh</u>*
	le canard *ler can-<u>ar</u>*
	la chèvre *lah shevr*

Dans la salle de classe - In the classroom

1 **La maîtresse** crie "Silence!"	1 **The teacher** calls "Silence!"
2 Chantal est sur **la chaise**.	2 Chantal is on **the chair**.
3 Pierre est sous **la table**.	3 Peter is under **the table**.
4 Mathieu jette **le livre**.	4 Matthew is throwing **the book**.
5 Elisabeth griffonne avec **les crayons de couleur**.	5 Elisabeth is scribbling with **the coloured pencils**.
6 Robert laisse tomber **la colle**.	6 Robert drops **the glue**.
7 Marie coupe **le papier**.	7 Mary is cutting up **the paper**.
8 **Le stylo** est sur **la table.**	8 **The pen** is on **the table**.
9 Et Paul joue tranquillement avec **l'ordinateur**!	9 And Paul is playing quietly with **the computer**!

la maîtresse

lah met-ress

la chaise

lah shez

la table

lah tabl'

le livre

ler leevr'

le crayon de couleur

ler cray-oh der cool-err

la colle

lah koll

le papier

ler papee-eh

le stylo

ler steelo

l'ordinateur

lordeenat-err

Touche ta tête - Touch your head

1	Je touche **ma tête**.	1	I'm touching **my head**.
2	Je touche **mes yeux**.	2	I'm touching **my eyes**.
3	Je touche **mon nez**.	3	I'm touching **my nose**.
4	Je touche **ma bouche**.	4	I'm touching **my mouth**.
5	Je touche **mes épaules**.	5	I'm touching **my shoulders**.
6	Je touche **mon bras**.	6	I'm touching **my arm**.
7	Je touche **ma main**.	7	I'm touching **my hand**.
8	Je touche **ma jambe**.	8	I'm touching **my leg**.
9	Je touche **mon pied**.	9	I'm touching **my foot**.

la tête

lah tet

les yeux

lez-yer

le nez

ler neh

la bouche

lah boosh

les épaules

lezeh-pol

le bras

ler brah

la main

lah mah

la jambe

lah shahmb

le pied

ler pee-eh

Dans la jungle - In the jungle

1	une coccinelle **rouge**		1	a **red** ladybird
2	un papillon **bleu**		2	a **blue** butterfly
3	une feuille **verte**		3	a **green** leaf
4	un fruit **jaune**		4	a **yellow** fruit
5	un perroquet **orange**		5	an **orange** parrot
6	une fourmi **noire**		6	a **black** ant
7	un papillon **blanc**		7	a **white** butterfly
8	une fleur **violette**		8	a **purple** flower
9	une branche **marron**		9	a **brown** branch

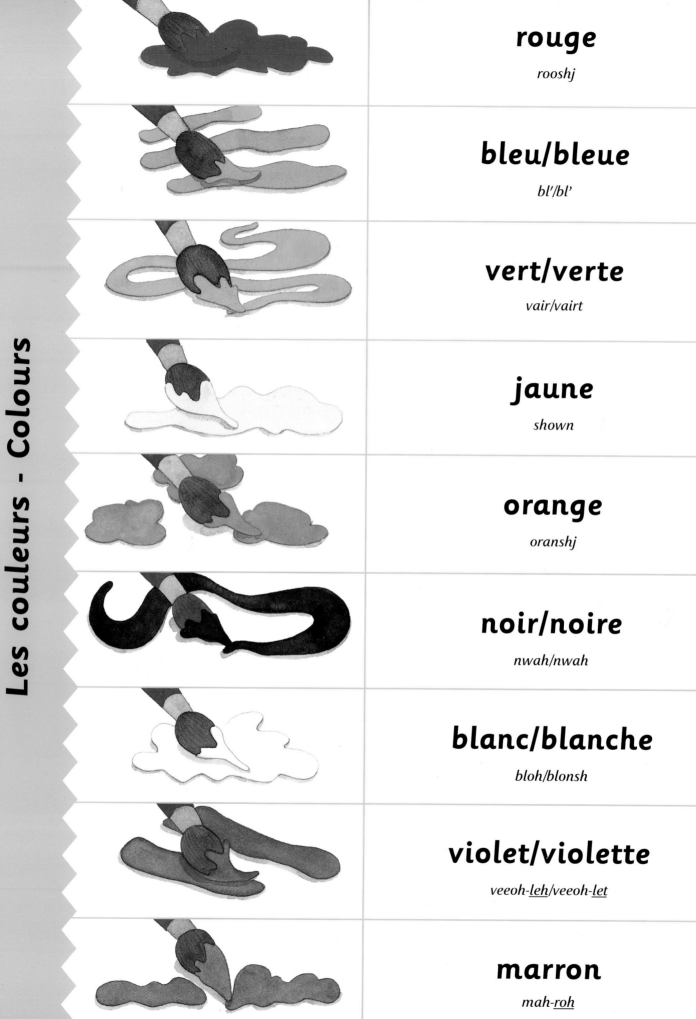

rouge

rooshj

bleu/bleue

bl'/bl'

vert/verte

vair/vairt

jaune

shown

orange

oranshj

noir/noire

nwah/nwah

blanc/blanche

bloh/blonsh

violet/violette

veeoh-leh/veeoh-let

marron

mah-roh

Le coffre à déguisement - The dressing-up box

1	Je mets **la jupe**.	1	I'm putting on **the skirt**.
2	Tu mets **la robe**?	2	Are you putting on **the dress**?
3	Caroline met **le pantalon**.	3	Caroline is putting on **the trousers**.
4	Jacques met **le manteau**.	4	Jack is putting on **the coat**.
5	Nous mettons **les chaussures**.	5	We're putting on **the shoes**.
6	Jean et Denis mettent **la chemise**.	6	John and Denis are putting on **the shirt**.
7	Claudine met **le pyjama**.	7	Claudine is putting on **the pyjamas**.
8	Le bébé met **les chaussettes**.	8	The baby is putting on **the socks**.
9	Le chien met **le chapeau**.	9	The dog is putting on **the hat**.

la jupe

lah shoop

la robe

lah rob

le pantalon

leh pantah-loh

le manteau

ler manto

les chaussures

leh showss-yoor

la chemise

lah sher-meez

le pyjama

ler peeshah-mah

les chaussettes

leh show-set

le chapeau

ler shapo

Une journée au zoo - A day at the zoo

1	**La girafe** a un petit.	1	**The giraffe** has a baby.
2	**Le lion** dort sous l'arbre.	2	**The lion** is sleeping under the tree.
3	**Le tigre** mange son repas.	3	**The tiger** is eating its meal.
4	**L'éléphant** se lave.	4	**The elephant** is washing.
5	**Le crocodile** nage dans le lac.	5	**The crocodile** is swimming in the lake.
6	**Le serpent** est dans l'arbre.	6	**The snake** is in the tree.
7	**L'ours blanc** grimpe sur un rocher.	7	**The polar bear** is climbing on a rock.
8	**L'hippopotame** aime la boue.	8	**The hippopotamus** likes mud.
9	**Le dauphin** saute en l'air.	9	**The dolphin** is jumping in the air.

la girafe

lah jeeraff

le lion

ler leeoh

le tigre

ler teegr'

l'éléphant

lelayfoh

le crocodile

ler krokodeel

le serpent

ler sairpoh

l'ours blanc

loors bloh

l'hippopotame

leepopotam

le dauphin

ler doh-fah

Dans la rue - In the street

1	La femme traverse **la rue**.	1	The woman is crossing **the street**.
2	Les enfants sont sur **le trottoir**.	2	The children are on **the pavement**.
3	**L'autobus** s'arrête à **l'arrêt d'autobus**.	3	**The bus** stops at **the bus stop**.
4	**Le camion** s'arrête **aux feux**.	4	**The lorry** stops at **the traffic lights**.
5	Le garçon est sur **la bicyclette**.	5	The boy is on **the bicycle**.
6	**La voiture** est rouge.	6	**The car** is red.
7	**La voiture de police** roule vite.	7	**The police car** is going fast.

la rue

lah roo

le trottoir

ler trotwah

l'autobus

low-toh-boos

l'arrêt d'autobus

larreh low-toh-boos

le camion

ler kamee-oh

les feux

leh fer

la bicyclette

lah beesee-klet

la voiture

lah vwot-yoor

la voiture de police

lah vwot-yoor der polees

15

À la plage - At the beach

1	**La mer** est bleue.	1	**The sea** is blue.
2	**Le sable** est jaune.	2	**The sand** is yellow.
3	**La mouette** mange **le poisson**.	3	**The seagull** is eating **the fish**.
4	**Les algues** sont vertes.	4	**The seaweed** is green.
5	**Le coquillage** est sur **le rocher**.	5	**The shell** is on **the rock**.
6	Les enfants sont dans **le voilier**.	6	The children are in **the sailing boat**.
7	Il y a beaucoup de grandes **vagues**.	7	There are lots of big **waves**.

la mer

lah mair

le sable

ler sabl'

la mouette

lah moo-et

le poisson

ler pwahssoh

les algues

lezalg

le coquillage

ler kokeeah-sh

le rocher

ler rosheh

le voilier

ler vwalee-eh

la vague

lah vag

17

Ma famille - My family

1 **Ma mère** est assise à la table.	1 **My mother** is sitting at the table.
2 **Mon père** parle avec **mon grand-père**.	2 **My father** is talking to **my grandfather**.
3 **Mon frère** joue avec son train.	3 **My brother** is playing with his train.
4 **Ma grand-mère** mange les spaghetti.	4 **My grandmother** is eating spaghetti.
5 **Ma tante** aide **ma sœur**.	5 **My aunt** is helping **my sister**.
6 **Mon oncle** boit de l'eau.	6 **My uncle** is drinking some water.
7 **Mes cousins** regardent la télévision.	7 **My cousins** are watching television.

La famille - The family

ma mère/maman
mah mair/ma<u>moh</u>

mon père/papa
moh pair/pa<u>pah</u>

ma sœur
mah sir

mon frère
moh frair

ma grand-mère
mah groh-<u>mair</u>

mon grand-père
moh groh-<u>pair</u>

ma tante
mah tohnt

mon oncle
mononkl'

mes cousins
meh koo<u>zah</u>

C'est la fête - Party time!

1 Sophie mange **un sandwich**.	1 Sophie is eating **a sandwich**.
2 Le bébé veut **du chocolat**.	2 The baby wants **some chocolate**.
3 **Le gâteau** est sur la table.	3 **The cake** is on the table.
4 **Les frites** sont chaudes!	4 **The chips** are hot!
5 **La pizza** est presque finie.	5 **The pizza** is almost finished.
6 Henri prend **une glace**.	6 Henry has **an ice-cream**.
7 Tu veux **du coca** ou **du jus d'orange**?	7 Do you want **coke** or **orange juice**?
8 Je préfère de **l'eau**.	8 I prefer **water**.

le sandwich

ler sondweech

le chocolat

ler shokolah

le gâteau

ler gatoh

les frites

leh freet

la pizza

lah peet-sah

la glace

lah glas

le coca

ler kokah

le jus d'orange

ler shoo d'oronsh

l'eau

loh

Acheter les jouets - Shopping for toys

1 **Le nounours** est plus grand que le garçon.

2 Alice joue avec **le robot**.

3 Olivier veut acheter **la balle**.

4 Tu préfères **le puzzle** ou **le jeu**?

5 **Le baby-foot** est vraiment marrant!

6 Carole et Guillaume regardent **le jeu-vidéo**.

7 Papa achète **la maquette d'avion**.

8 Les filles aiment **les perles**.

1 **The teddy** is bigger than the boy.

2 Alice is playing with **the robot**.

3 Oliver wants to buy **the ball**.

4 Do you prefer **the puzzle** or **the game**?

5 **Table football** is really fun!

6 Carol and William are looking at **the computer game**.

7 Dad is buying **the model aeroplane kit**.

8 The girls like **the beads**.

le nounours

ler noo-noorss

le robot

ler roh-boh

la balle

lah bal

le puzzle

ler pooz-leh

le jeu

ler sher

le baby-foot

ler baby-foot

le jeu-vidéo

ler sher veedeh-oh

la maquette d'avion

lah maket davee-oh

les perles

leh pairl

Faire la vaisselle - Washing up

1. Papa fait la vaisselle dans **l'évier**.
2. Maman coupe la pomme avec **le couteau**.
3. **La cuillère** et **la fourchette** sont sales.
4. Julie prend **un verre** d'eau.
5. Le chat regarde dans **le frigo**!
6. **L'assiette** tombe.
7. **Les casseroles** sont sur **la cuisinière**.

1. Daddy is washing up in **the sink**.
2. Mummy is cutting the apple with **the knife**.
3. **The spoon** and **the fork** are dirty.
4. Julie has **a glass** of water.
5. The cat is looking in **the fridge**!
6. **The plate** is falling down.
7. **The saucepans** are on **the cooker**.

l'évier

lev-eeh

le couteau

ler kootoh

la cuillère

lah kwee-air

la fourchette

lah foor-shet

le verre

ler vair

le frigo

ler free-goh

l'assiette

lassee-et

la casserole

lah kasserol

la cuisinière

lah kweezeen-yair

À la campagne - In the country

1	Hélène monte dans **l'arbre**.	1	Helen is climbing **the tree**.
2	**L'herbe** est verte.	2	**The grass** is green.
3	**Le champ** est plein de **fleurs**.	3	**The field** is full of **flowers**.
4	**La montagne** est très haute.	4	**The mountain** is very high.
5	Il y a beaucoup **d'arbres** dans **la forêt**.	5	There are a lot of **trees** in **the forest**.
6	**Le pont** enjambe **la rivière**.	6	**The bridge** crosses **the river**.
7	**L'oiseau** fait son nid.	7	**The bird** is making its nest.

l'arbre

larbr'

l'herbe

lairb

le champ

ler shom

la fleur

lah fler

la montagne

lah mon<u>tyn-y</u>'

la forêt

lah for<u>eh</u>

le pont

ler pon

la rivière

lah reevee-<u>air</u>

l'oiseau

lwuz-<u>oh</u>

L'heure du bain - Bathtime

1 Guy se lave avec **le savon**.	1 Guy is washing himself with **the soap**.
2 **Le lavabo** est plein d'eau.	2 **The washbasin** is full of water.
3 Luc joue avec **la douche**.	3 Luke is playing with **the shower**.
4 Le chat dort sur **la serviette**.	4 The cat is sleeping on **the towel**.
5 **Les cabinets** sont à côté de la baignoire.	5 **The toilet** is next to **the bath**.
6 Madeleine met **le dentifrice** sur la brosse à dents.	6 Madeleine is putting **toothpaste** on the toothbrush.
7 **Le miroir** est au-dessus **du lavabo**.	7 **The mirror** is above **the washbasin**.

le savon

ler sa<u>voh</u>

le lavabo

ler lava<u>boh</u>

la douche

lah doosh

la serviette

lah sairvee-<u>et</u>

les cabinets

leh kabeen-<u>eh</u>

la baignoire

lah beyn-<u>nwah</u>

le dentifrice

ler dontee-<u>frees</u>

la brosse à dents

lah bross ah <u>dohn</u>

le miroir

ler meer<u>wah</u>

Dans ma chambre - In my bedroom

1 Je dors dans **mon lit**.	1 I'm sleeping in **my bed**.
2 **Le réveil** est sur **l'étagère**.	2 **The alarm clock** is on **the shelf**.
3 J'aime regarder **la télévision**.	3 I like watching **television**.
4 **Mon lit** est près de **la fenêtre**.	4 **My bed** is near **the window**.
5 Mes vêtements sont dans **mon armoire**.	5 My clothes are in **the wardrobe**.
6 **Mon Walkman** est sur **le tapis**.	6 **My Walkman** is on **the rug**.
7 Maman ouvre **la porte**.	7 Mummy is opening **the door**.

La chambre - The bedroom

le lit

ler lee

le réveil

ler reh-vay

l'étagère

letah-shair

la télévision

lah teh-lehveezeeoh

la fenêtre

lah f'nair-tr'

l'armoire

larm-wah

le Walkman

ler wokman

le tapis

ler tapee

la porte

lah port

31

Word list

À la ferme p. 2 — On the farm
Les animaux de la ferme — Farm animals

le canard	duck
le chat	cat
le cheval	horse
la chèvre	goat
le chien	dog
le cochon	pig
le mouton	sheep
la souris	mouse
la vache	cow

Dans la salle de classe p. 4 — In the classroom
La salle de classe — The classroom

la chaise	chair
la colle	glue
le crayon de couleur	coloured pencil
le livre	book
le papier	paper
la maîtresse	teacher
l'ordinateur	computer
le stylo	pen
la table	table

Touche ta tête p. 6 — Touch your head
Le corps — The body

la bouche	mouth
le bras	arm
les épaules	shoulders
la jambe	leg
la main	hand
le nez	nose
le pied	foot
la tête	head
les yeux	eyes

Dans la jungle p. 8 — In the jungle
Les couleurs — Colours

blanc/blanche	white
bleu/bleue	blue
jaune	yellow
marron	brown
noir/noire	black
orange	orange
rouge	red
vert/verte	green
violet/violette	purple

Le coffre à déguisement p. 10 — The dressing-up box
Les vêtements — Clothes

le chapeau	hat
les chaussettes	socks
les chaussures	shoes
la chemise	shirt
la jupe	skirt
le manteau	coat
le pantalon	trousers
le pyjama	pyjamas
la robe	dress

Une journée au zoo p. 12 — A day at the zoo
Les animaux sauvages — Wild animals

le crocodile	crocodile
le dauphin	dolphin
l'éléphant	elephant
la girafe	giraffe
l'hippopotame	hippopotamus
le lion	lion
l'ours blanc	polar bear
le serpent	snake
le tigre	tiger

Dans la rue p. 14 — In the street
La rue — The street

l'arrêt d'autobus	bus stop
l'autobus	bus
la bicyclette	bicycle
le camion	lorry
les feux	traffic lights
la rue	street
le trottoir	pavement
la voiture	car
la voiture de police	police car

À la plage p. 16 — At the beach
La plage — The beach

les algues	seaweed
le coquillage	shell
la mer	sea
la mouette	seagull
le poisson	fish
le rocher	rock
le sable	sand
la vague	wave
le voilier	sailing boat

Ma famille p. 18 — My family
La famille — The family

mes cousins	cousins
mon frère	brother
ma grand-mère	grandmother
mon grand-père	grandfather
ma mère/maman	mother/mummy
mon oncle	uncle
mon père/papa	father/daddy
ma sœur	sister
ma tante	aunt

C'est la fête p. 20 — Party time!
La fête — The party

le chocolat	chocolate
le coca	coke
l'eau	water
les frites	chips
le gâteau	cake
la glace	ice-cream
le jus d'orange	orange juice
la pizza	pizza
le sandwich	sandwich

Acheter les jouets p. 22 — Shopping for toys
Les jouets — Toys

le baby-foot	table football
la balle	ball
le jeu	game
le jeu-vidéo	computer game
la maquette d'avion	model aeroplane kit
le nounours	teddy
les perles	beads
le puzzle	puzzle
le robot	robot

Faire la vaisselle p. 24 — Washing up
La cuisine — The kitchen

l'assiette	plate
la casserole	saucepan
le couteau	knife
la cuillère	spoon
la cuisinière	cooker
l'évier	sink
la fourchette	fork
le frigo	fridge
le verre	glass

À la campagne p. 26 — In the country
La campagne — The country

l'arbre	tree
le champ	field
la fleur	flower
la forêt	forest
l'herbe	grass
la montagne	mountain
l'oiseau	bird
le pont	bridge
la rivière	river

L'heure du bain p. 28 — Bathtime
La salle de bains — The bathroom

la baignoire	bath
la brosse à dents	toothbrush
les cabinets	toilet
le dentifrice	toothpaste
la douche	shower
le lavabo	washbasin
le miroir	mirror
le savon	soap
la serviette	towel

Dans ma chambre p. 30 — In my bedroom
La chambre — The bedroom

l'armoire	wardrobe
l'étagère	shelf
la fenêtre	window
le lit	bed
la porte	door
le réveil	alarm clock
le tapis	rug
la télévision	television
le Walkman	Walkman